(*Cover*) Wine bowl from Southern Italy: comedy scene with lover climbing ladder to girl at window (cf. Aristophanes, *Ecclesiazousae*) 360–340 BC.

(*Left*) Slave seated on altar where he has taken refuge, mockingly raising hand to ear as though he cannot hear his pursuer shouting at him to leave it. Greek terracotta statuette made in Athens about 350 BC.

Weird masks, outlandish characters, h
posing or shifting about the stage in
movements – these are probably the im
when they hear of 'the Greek theatre'.
and remote form of entertainment, b
production of a Greek drama to see the
appreciate the impact of the tragedy, and the hilarity of the comedy.

The basic conventions of the Greek theatre, variously refined and modified through the ages, still form the principles of our modern theatre. Even the words that we use – theatre, drama, scene, programme, orchestra – though some are now slightly changed in meaning, have been derived from the Greek. Not only are the ancient plays still performed in their own right, in both local and national theatres, but updated versions have always been popular. The Roman playwrights Plautus and Terence, the French dramatists Racine and Molière and our own Shakespeare, to name but a few, have all borrowed material, in the way of plots, themes or characters, from the Greek drama. Even today, farces like *A Funny Thing Happened on the Way to the Forum* owe a great deal to these ancient productions.

Where the ancient theatre differed very much from ours was in the part that it played in people's lives. Fortunately for us, both the Greeks and the Romans so enjoyed the theatre that they even decorated their household wares with representations from it. We find theatrical masks gracing the handles of bronze bowls and on terracotta lamps, scenes from plays pictured on bowls for mixing wine, wall paintings and floor mosaics, and masks made of stone, bronze and clay used as hanging decorations for the home. Tiny masks shaped in gold and others in the form of glass pendants

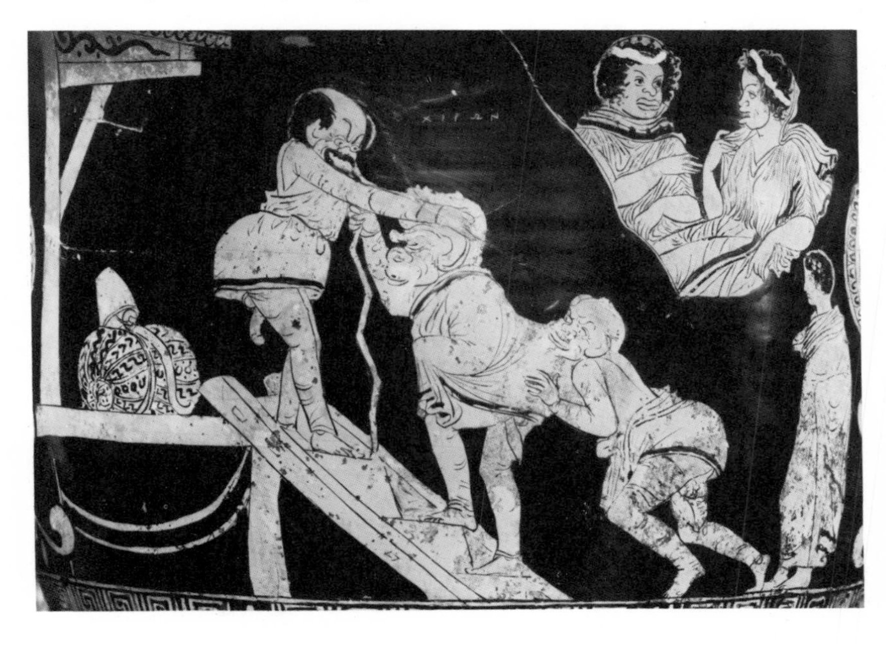

Parody of the myth of Cheiron (the centaur, enacted by an old man with a slave pushing from behind). The slave Xanthias helps him from further up the stairs leading into the 'Temple of Apollo' where Cheiron goes to be cured of blindness. *Top right:* two nymphs. *Below:* Achilles. Wine-bowl, made in Southern Italy about 380 BC.

(*Above*) Greek and Roman objects decorated with theatrical masks: carved finger ring, bone mask from a hairpin, bronze mask from a vase.

(*Left*) Parody of an incident in Homer. Dolon ambushed by Odysseus and Diomedes. Wine bowl made in Southern Italy, about 390–380 BC.

Dionysos in his ship-cart. Reconstructed drawing from vase made in Athens about 500 BC.

were used as jewellery, and minute ones were used as seal-stones in finger rings. The Greeks also collected sets of terracotta statuettes representing the characters of their favourite plays: in contrast, we can hardly imagine anyone nowadays adorning their shelves with figures from plays.

Drama and Religion

To the Greeks, the importance of the theatre lay not in that it was a mere entertainment, but that it was a performance very closely associated with religion. It was not a round-the-year commercial entertainment, but took place only once annually; at Athens, for example, drama was part of the great festival which was held at the end of every March, and called the City Dionysia. The celebration was in honour of Dionysos, the god of wine and laughter, who was believed to bring back spring to the countryside. An image of Dionysos, or perhaps a priest dressed as the god, was carried around the city and its outskirts in a ship-cart, accompanied by a joyous procession of people singing and dancing. Such festivities and religious ceremonies went on for three days; the next four days saw the most exciting event–the play contest. Playwrights and actors competed for prizes just like the athletes and musicians at other Greek national festivals–the games at Olympia, Delphi and Athens.

Everyone in Athens whose work allowed him to do so went along to the theatre of Dionysos to attend the performances on all four days. The state paid for any citizen too poor to afford admission. Separate blocks of seats were allotted to each district or tribe of a city. Athens had ten tribes and some of the theatre tickets that survive, small bronze or lead discs, display amongst other symbols the name of one of the tribes, Erechtheus.

The Production of the Plays

The oranization of the dramatic competitions was serious state business. When the *archon* (the annually elected chief-magistrate) took up office at the beginning of July, he chose three rich men to produce the tragedies, and five more to produce the comedies at the next City Dionysia. These sponsors were called *choregoi* (literally, 'chorus-leaders'). Their task was considered a great privilege. Each choregos might have to provide up to 5000 drachmas (roughly equal to ten years' wages for the average man) to finance items such as the rehearsals of the cast, training, payment of musicians, masks, costumes, and so on. The archon also chose three tragic poets and five comic poets out of those who submitted plays, or at least outlines of plays, for consideration. The comic poets produced only one comedy each, but the tragic poets presented three tragedies linked in theme and called a 'trilogy', and also a type of burlesque called a satyr-play. The archon was perhaps also responsible for allotting a troupe of three actors to each dramatist for the actors were paid by the state, while the main concern of the choregos was the chorus. The tragedies were performed on the first three days, and the comedies on the last day.

Marble thrones for priests and officials in the theatre of Dionysos at Athens. The front row was sheltered by a canopy resting on wooden posts. 4th century BC.

At the end of each day the judges, who had special thrones in the front row of the theatre, wrote their decisions on clay tablets; the first play chosen by five judges was the winner. There was another competition for the best actor. The prizes for the poets were first a bull, second a large jar (*amphora*) full of wine, and third a goat. The victorious chorus won a bronze tripod and cauldron with ring-handles, which was duly dedicated to Dionysos and set up in the Street of the Tripods, an impressive thoroughfare lined with these monuments. The choregoi themselves often made dedications for the privilege of holding office, like the monument of the choregos Lysicrates, a tiny circular temple of Dionysos still standing in Athens, or the now headless statue of a Muse in the British Museum. Sometimes they also gave banquets for their chorus, and wine bowls specially made for the occasion have survived which show the actors feasting, with their names inscribed beside them.

The Origins of Greek Drama

Satyr-play. We have already seen that one type of play performed at the City Dionysia was a satyr-play. Satyrs were traditionally the wild followers of Dionysos–mischievous creatures with snub-noses, goats' ears and horses' tails. Their revels and antics formed a delightful and sometimes bawdy entertainment. This section of the drama was in fact the oldest surviving element of the festival. It is interesting that the cult of Dionysos, which arrived in Greece from the East, was banished by most of the other Greek cities, who despised the wild rites performed by the disciples of Dionysos while drunk on wine, the gift of the god. But the Athenians

Satyrs revelling, the leader dressed as Hermes, with herald's staff and travelling hat. Wine-cooler made in Athens about 490–480 BC.

assimilated the performances into their own dramatic contests and made them one of the most outstanding features of Athenian social life.

The satyr revellers can be traced back at least as far as the seventh century BC when we find representations on vases from the Peloponnese of ribald dancers in padded costumes who seem to have performed mockeries of the tales of the heroes and of daily life. These farces were introduced into Attica and combined with the local band of merry-makers (the *komos*) who sang and danced fertility rites at the country festival of Dionysos. At this time there was no theatre, just a circular clearing probably near to a temple of Dionysos, where the religious followers performed. No doubt the ground was originally a threshing floor, a further connection between the harvest and Dionysos as a fertility god. Arion, a poet in the court of Periander, tyrant of Corinth in the late seventh century BC, is credited with being the inventor of the *dithyramb*, the formal version of the Dionysiac song and dance which had long been in existence, and he gave the satyr-costume to the singers of the dithyramb. From this chorus developed the satyr-play, which by the late sixth century was presented at the festival after the three related tragedies.

The daring improvisations of the komos sometimes directed ridicule and obscenity at the spectators, and therefore the performers had resorted to masks and disguises for anonymity. The wild nature of the rites made it natural for some of these costumes to be in the form of animals, and the choruses of wasps, birds, and frogs which we find in the comedies of Aristophanes in the fifth and early fourth centuries BC are remnants of these early entertainers. So too is the ridicule and accusations which are heaped upon the politics, manners and thought of the Athenian people.

Certain stock characters from the Peloponnesian parodies were also retained – such as the comic version of Hercules, the roistering old man and the impudent slave girl. On occasions episodes in the life of Dionysos, the original theme of the revels, were still performed.

Tragedy. Unlikely though it seems, tragedy was an offshoot of the satyr-plays. 'Tragos' meant 'one who dresses up and performs as a follower of Dionysos'. The goat was the sacred animal of Dionysos, and hence the satyr's goat-like appearance. A goat was also given as a third prize at the dramatic festivals, as we have seen.

According to the Greek writer Aristotle, tragedy developed from the dithyramb. It probably began to take shape when the subjects of the dithyramb became more varied; eventually there emerged one actor from the throng who discarded the satyr mask and assumed the costume of the individual whom he impersonated. Thespis is said to have created the first actor set in opposition to the chorus, about 534 BC, during the reign of the tyrant Peisistratos.

In the early fifth century BC, the tragedian Aeschylus created a second actor to permit freer development of the dialogue, and then Sophocles invented a third. Meanwhile the chorus, usually about fifteen in number, diminished in importance, and drama of a recognizably modern type evolved.

But the chief difference between ancient and modern drama lies in the music. The chorus was always accompanied by a musician on the double-pipes, to which they danced and the lines of the play were intoned. The

Terracotta statuettes made in Athens of actors in stock character roles: 'woman' with veil coyly pulled over face, Hercules, flirtatious girl.

double-pipes (*aulos*) had been used as far back as the seventh century BC to accompany sacrifices, processions, and chorus singing and dancing.

Drama had in fact developed from poetry and song. It used the material of the traditional epic poems, particularly Homer's *Iliad* and *Odyssey*, and the music of the lyric (lyric means the song to the accompaniment of the lyre). The marble relief by the sculptor Archelaos of Priene is carved with figures who personify these elements.

Before about 480 BC, only mythological subjects were represented, but then Phrynichus, a pupil of Thespis, produced the first historic dramas. Though the events were no longer remote in time, they were still remote in place. Several of the early historic plays were located in Persia: for example, Phrynichus' *Capture of Miletus* and Aeschylus' *Persians*. Phrynichus' *Phoenician Women* depicting the defeat of the second Persian invasion of Greece in 480–479 BC was first performed in 476–475 BC with the statesman Themistocles as choregos. It has even been suggested that the first stage background to be used was the tent of Xerxes, captured in the Persian defeat; it could have formed a background for many dramas and in its grandeur probably resembled Persian palace architecture.

According to Aristotle, the tragic play fulfilled a purpose, namely to purge the emotions by means of pity and fear. This revitalizing experience is very much akin to the effect of a religious ceremony. Tragedy was also believed to be a means of instruction, encouraging citizens to excel in virtue both in public and private life. Sophocles is said to have been appointed one of the generals in the expedition to Samos (440 BC) on account of political wisdom shown in certain passages of his *Antigone*.

Sophocles. Greek bronze head from a statue. Made about 300–200 BC.

Small jug showing flute-player with chorus of men dressed up as cocks; the vine sprays show that they are performing in honour of Dionysos. 500–480 BC.

Comedy. It is easy to understand how comedy was developed from satyr performances. Again, several actors were gradually set up in opposition to the chorus.

Whereas Athenian tragedy had attained its final form by the end of the fifth century BC, so that the fourth century simply saw the revival of the great tragedies of earlier days, the development of Athenian comedy continued. It is separated into three distinct phases. 'Old Comedy' coincides with the great period of Athenian tragedy, and culminated in the works of Aristophanes. By this time the political life of Athens began to deteriorate; when it was no longer an independent democracy, and free speech was curtailed, lampoons of public life became less appropriate, and the petty vices of private life and individuals were chosen for ridicule. 'Middle Comedy', which belonged to the fourth century BC, retained the old actor types.

Most of the terracotta and bronze statuettes which illustrate these characters belong to the period 400–350 BC, since grotesque forms and exaggerated features were not popular in Athens in the preceding years, when the city was at its height of artistic achievement. While some of these figures were no doubt sold individually others must have been made and sold in a complete set, to represent the cast of a play. Two such sets are now in the Metropolitan Museum, New York; they came from a tomb in Athens, where they were probably placed as favourite possessions of the dead man. Two similar examples are illustrated; one is an actor playing the part of a woman, since, just as in the Elizabethan theatre, there were no actresses, and the other is a stock comic character, a slave who has run away and taken sanctuary on an altar. The hand raised mockingly to his ear indicates that he is deaf to appeals to leave the safety of the altar.

In the 'New Comedy' the cumbersome padded costumes were discarded and everyday clothes were adopted. The outstanding writer of the period was Menander, whose numerous plays date from the fourth and early third centuries BC. In thirty-three years, he wrote more than one hundred comedies. Once established, New Comedy became a tradition which lasted several centuries, through the Roman revivals of Plautus and Terence.

Drama in Southern Italy

The Greek colonies of Southern Italy and Sicily took over the form of tragedy already performed in the homeland. Aeschylus visited Sicily, wrote plays there, and eventually died there in exile. There is a vast ancient theatre in Syracuse, largely rebuilt in Roman times; here it was in 413 BC that the old men and women of Syracuse crowded to watch the fight in the harbour below, and saw their own ships win victory over the invading Athenians. The Roman biographer Plutarch tells how the Athenian prisoners were saved because of the esteem felt for Euripides in Sicily; some were given food and drink for repeating his verses, and others were released from slavery for teaching their masters some of his passages. But the Western Greeks had their own type of comedy. This was a mime, in which there were presented burlesques of mythology and daily life. Later the legendary tales of the heroes also became the subject of parody. The master of this form of entertainment was said to be Rhinthon, who perfected it in about 300 BC. The actors are called *phlyakes* or gossips. and they are pictured on numerous South Italian vases. Their padded costumes are similar to those of the Old Comedy, and judging from the scenes represented, the performances were racy and uproarious.

Costume

Masks. Masks were not the original form of facial disguise used for dramatic performances. The creative Thespis (see page 6) is said to have treated his actors' faces with white lead, then covered them with cinnabar (a red oxide of mercury) or rubbed them with wine lees, and then he finally introduced masks of unpainted linen. His successor Choerilus made further experiments with masks, which would have been made of clay, or stiffened linen, cork or wood. Phrynichus is said to have introduced women's masks; this may mean that he was the first to have his chorus appear as women. All ancient actors, leaders and chorus members, were men.

Effects of misfortune sometimes made necessary a change to a fresh mask: Helen, in Euripides' *Helen*, for example, returns to the stage with

(*Above left*) Tragic mask of Hercules

(*Above right*) Mask of the young Dionysos.

(*See also inside back cover.*)

hair cut off and pale cheeks; Oedipus, in the *Oedipus Tyrannus* of Sophocles, is seen with blood-stained face and blinded eyes.

Masks covering the whole head were of course worn by all the participants in the satyr-plays; the 'Pronomos vase' in Naples, called after the flute-player whose name is inscribed beside him on the vase, shows members of the chorus carrying satyr masks just like those of the satyrs revelling on the other side of the vase.

The use of large masks, with their exaggerated features, enabled the whole audience to see the characters more clearly. It also allowed the actors to change parts more quickly, for while the leading actor had only one part, his assistants might have up to six roles to play; sometimes in the comedies they had less than ten seconds to change parts. There is a statuette in Vienna of an old woman with grinning mouth holding the laughing mask of a young man, who must represent an actor in the midst of changing roles.

The most striking feature of the masks is their huge, trumpet-shaped mouth (see page 2). They are always wide open, allowing the actor's voice to come through clearly, and giving an impression of continual communication; the masks of the mime actors on the other hand always had their lips sealed. It used to be thought that the trumpet-mouths increased the volume of the voice, but recent experiments have proved this to be untrue. The theatres have such marvellous acoustics that a whisper uttered from the orchestra can be heard right up to the highest tier, without any aid at all.

The faces on various types of mask soon became traditional and remained almost unchanged for centuries. Pollux, writing in the second century AD, enumerates twenty-eight types of mask; the principal features of the different masks are mainly distinguished from one another by the style of the hair, the colour of the complexion, the height of the hairstyle, and the expression of the eyes. The *onkos* style of hair-dressing found in some of the tragic masks (see page 2) preserves a fashion dating from around 500 BC, in which the long tresses of hair were brought forward and piled up in curls over the brow.

Another persistent feature of male masks, particularly in comedy, is the pointed beard cut in the form of a wedge, a fashion originating in the period of the Persian wars. To judge from surviving marble and bronze portraits, Aeschylus seems to have worn this type of beard.

Dress. Like the mask, the rest of the actor's costume was all-important in signifying identity and character to the audience.

The tragic actor's apparel was grand and elaborate. The colour and music of the theatre must have formed a splendid spectacle.

The setting of some of the early tragedies in the land of Persia provided the opportunity for colourfully ornamented and embroidered costume. Along with Dionysos, the goddesses of the Eleusinian Mystery cults, Demeter and Persephone, who also originated in the East, are often

Demeter, wearing elaborately decorated oriental costume similar to that worn by tragic actors. From cup made in Athens about 490–480 BC.

depicted in this type of robe. Dionysos also sometimes appears wearing the tall hunting boot, from which the *cothurni*, boots with high, brightly painted platform soles, were derived.

Aeschylus is credited with the introduction of most of the outstanding features of the actor's costume. The further enlargement of masks, onkoi and cothurni towards the end of the fourth century BC seems to indicate that tragic actors moved less and less around the stage, and relied increasingly upon expression of voice and elaborate gestures. This was incidentally very wise, since the perilous height of the shoes and weight of the masks must have put actors in grave danger of falling off the stage, if they ventured too close to the edge.

The dress of the tragic actors was similar to that of everyday life – a long tunic over which was worn a thick cloak – but more flowing and dignified. The actors wore padding uniformly over the body, so that the stature of the figure was altogether increased. The broad girdle worn by the tragic actor high up under the breast no doubt helped to keep the padding in place.

The costume of the comic actors, on the other hand, was, and was intended to be, quite ridiculous. The body was grotesquely padded and enclosed in a tight-fitting undergarment, such as we might call a body-stocking. This was usually dyed flesh-colour or red, but was sometimes decorated with stripes. Over the unwieldy body a short tunic was worn, and, until the New Comedy of about 330 BC, it was just too short to be decent. The arms and legs had to be left free for the actors to caper and cavort about the stage, but their clumsiness and any over-balancing would have contributed to the general fun (see illustrations on pages 1, 6, front cover and inside front cover).

Architecture

The plan of the ancient Greek theatre corresponds with the three elements of ancient drama – the circular orchestra for the chorus who provided dancing and music, the stage for the actors who presented the words, and the fan-shaped auditorium for the spectators.

The auditorium was usually cut into the slope of a hill, and the sides of the hollow were faced with stone or marble seating, and divided into sections by gangways. Usually there was seating for as many as 18,000.

It seems that the plays were always performed to a full house; Plato mentions one audience of 30,000, and Aristophanes jokes that once the performance had started, the only way to get out of the theatre was to sprout wings.

All Greek theatres had circular orchestras, or dancing places, as excavations at Epidauros, Eretria, Sicyon, Megalopolis, Amphiraeus and Delphi have shown. In the centre or at the side of the orchestra there stood an altar, or *thymele*, dedicated to Dionysos; at Epidauros a circular plaque marks where this stood. Both the orchestra and altar are relics of the followers of Dionysos who performed dithyrambic dances and songs around the altar of the god. Most of the surviving Greek plays were written in the 5th century BC. At that time no part of the theatre was made of stone except for the foundations. The seats and stage were made of wood, and the floor was beaten earth or turf (see page 5). The stone theatres that we see today in parts of Greece date from the fourth century BC onwards, but the form was the same, the structure merely being made more permanent by the use of stone or marble. When the chorus lost some of its importance in Roman times, part of the orchestra was forfeited and an oblong stage was added. The whole of the stage building was called the *skene*, from which we derive our word scenery. The simple background of the stage must have made the actors in their colourful costumes stand out rather like the painted sculpture on a temple frieze. The narrow stage probably limited the movement of the actors, but we have already noted that the impact of the drama relied on spectacle, measured gestures and voice production.

In the fourth century the stage consisted of two floors; the lower, called the *proscenium*, had an entrance on either side, approached by ramps, while the upper floor or *hyposcenium* was decorated with paintings and surrounded by columns. The whole stage structure was roofed and walled and had three gates, like the façade of a palace or temple.

The first production for which these features were necessary was the *Orestaia* of Aeschylus, first performed in the year 458 BC. Most plays were set in a public square in front of a palace or temple, as though an important event in the life of a city were taking place before the spectators. The central doorway was the royal gate through which the leading actor (*protagonist*, literally 'first contestant') entered, while the right-hand gate led to the guest chamber and that on the left to the sanctuary. The two side

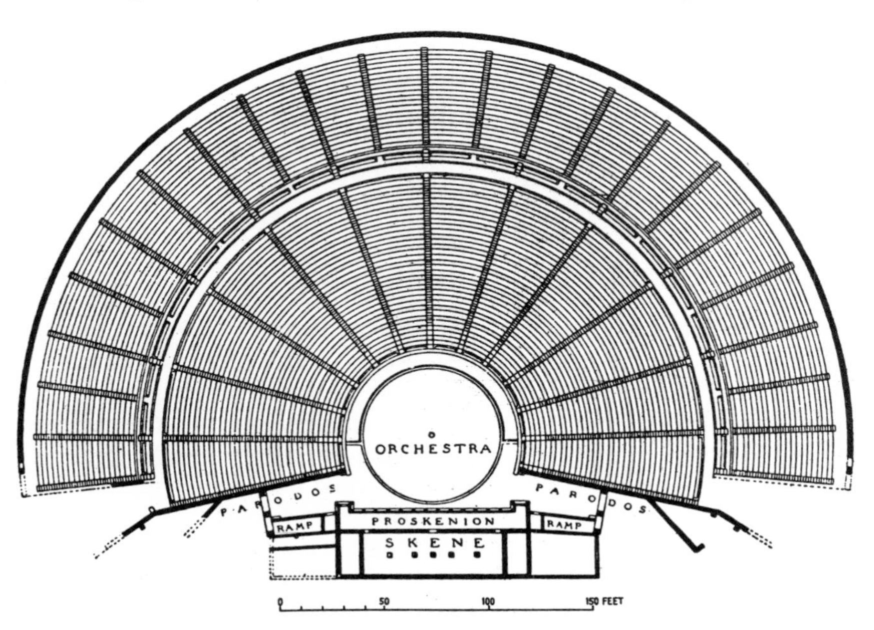

Plan of the theatre at Epidauros as it was constructed in the 4th century BC.

entrances also had their own conventional purposes – that on the right led to the countryside and the left to the city.

In Roman times, the authors Vitruvius and Pollux wrote detailed accounts of the ancient stage settings and scenery. Although it is difficult to determine how much of their evidence relates to the Roman and not the Greek theatre, they are both known to have derived information from earlier sources, and much of their writings must hold good. For example, their descriptions sometimes agree with the scanty remains of the classical theatres, or scenes painted on vases, and they describe devices known from extant fifth-century plays.

Before about 340 BC, background scenery consisted merely of a temporary structure leaning against the front wall of the building at the back of the stage which was probably used by the actors for changing, or storing scenery. In the beginning the backdrop was merely a framework of wood covered in skins, which were dried and tinted red. Such screens were first painted with pictures in the time of Aeschylus. It is interesting that this early scenery, painted by the artist Agatharchus, inspired philosophers to do the first research into perspective. It is Sophocles who is credited with the invention of scenery painting (*skenographia*). The backdrops are called by Pollux *katablemata*, or throw-overs, referring to the fact that they could be very quickly changed, or placed one over the other, during the short intermissions between the four plays which took place on each festival day. The katablemata might also be attached to the structures in the wings of the stage, which Pollux and Vitruvius described as prisms, differently decorated on each of the three sides, and capable of being rotated to indicate a different locality. Thus scenery for the four plays of the day could be easily accommodated on the prisms, the fourth backdrop being changed with the first during one of the performances.

Where the scenery failed to convince, there were always the brilliant descriptions of the dramatists to supplement the audience's imagination: a fine example is the opening scene of Aeschylus' *Agamemnon* where the herald describes the flaring beacons in the blackness of night (the audience of course was in broad daylight) that announce the victory and homecoming of the king.

Devices

The most important device of the ancient theatre was the movable platform, or *ekkyklema*. Its purpose was to reveal an event inside the building. It consisted of either a rectangular platform which could be wheeled out through the doors of the stage-building or a rotatable circular platform, pivoted in the centre, with a screen across the diameter to fit the corresponding gap in the stage wall. It was a favourite device of Euripides who employed it, for example, in his *Hippolytos* when Phaedra is shown on a couch. It was particularly useful for revealing a murdered corpse, as in Aeschylus' *Agamemnon*.

A more astounding spectacle was created by the 'flying machine' a

A scene from Euripides' *Oineus. From left to right:* Oineus, Periboia, Diomedes before an altar on which is the helpless Agrios, with a Fury rising up beside him (perhaps by means of the trap-door in the stage-floor). Wine-jar made in Southern Italy, about 340–330 BC.

crane behind the scenes which enabled characters to fly through the air. It was another device favoured by Euripides and he made ample use of it for his *deus ex machina*, (god out of a machine), who often appeared over the scene at the end of his plays. Aristophanes delights in parodying this piece of machinery; in his *Peace*, the character Trygaios flies to heaven on a dung-beetle and appeals to the stage-hand not to let him fall.

A useful means of producing a ghostly apparition was an underground passage leading to a trap door, enabling the figure to materialize suddenly before the audience. This would be used, for example, for the ghost of Darius in Aeschylus' *Persians*, or that of Clytemnestra in the *Eumenides*. It may be referred to on a vase painting depicting Euripides' *Oineus*, where a black Fury or demon is rising up beside the altar.

There must have been various other props and devices used by the ancient dramatist. In Aristophanes' *Frogs*, for example, the orchestra is supposed to be a lake full of frogs (the chorus), through which Dionysos rows a small boat, presumably one on wheels with a hole in the bottom through which he could propel the boat forward with his feet.

Sound-effects. The Greeks, not surprisingly, were also very resourceful when it came to creating sound effects. There were, for example, numerous ways to represent thunder, which would have been amplified by the excellent acoustics: pebbles were poured out of a jar into a large bronze vessel, bags were filled with stones and flung against a metal surface, or lead balls were dropped on a sheet of tightly stretched leather. There was an amusing way of providing lighting: a plank, with a flash of lightning painted on a dark background, was shot out of a box into a receptacle below.

Marble relief showing (*top*) Zeus with Mnemosyne (Memory), and (*below*) their children – the nin Muses. At the bottom is Homer enthroned in his sanctuary like a god, with figures representing the Iliad and Odysse kneeling beside him. The masked figures on the rig are Tragedy and Comedy, amid other personifica-tions. The relief shows that all literary forms we thought to have originated with Homer. Greek, carved about 300–200 BC by Archelaos of Priene.

(*Right*) Tragic mask of hero.

(*Back cover*) The theatre at Dodo 3rd century BC. Like other Greel theatres, it was i magnificent natural setting. (Photo: R. G. Broomfield).

Further Reading

The History of the Greek and Roman Theatre, M. Bieber (Princeton University Press 1961)

Greek Theatre Production, T. B. L. Webster (Methuen 1956)

Illustrations of Greek Drama, A. D. Trendall and T. B. L. Webster (Phaidon 1971)

The Attic Theatre, A. E. Haigh (Oxford 1907)

Published by British Museum Publications Limited, 6 Bedf Square, London WC1B 3RA

Designed by Jar Shurmer

ISBN 0 7141 00

Printed in Engla by Martin Cadbury, Worcester